The Exciting, Social & Emotional Adventures of chatting

TIMMY!

爱聊天的提米之精彩的社交与情感奇遇

MAKING A FRIEND

交朋友

Dr. Ira N. B. Canada

Hi friends! Remember my playground experience, where I
wanted to make a friend, but was unable?

朋友们好！还记得我在游乐场想交个朋友却没
成功的经历吗？

Good morning Mom. I'm excited to go to school today because Mr. Canada is going to show us how to make a friend!

妈妈，早上好。今天我很期待去学校，因为加拿大老师要教我们怎么交朋友！

I'm excited because I want to be able to make friends at school and in my neighborhood or elsewhere.

我很兴奋，因为我想要在学校交朋友，也想在我的小区和别的地方交朋友。

Good morning class. We had a great "Check Yourself" this morning! Now I'm going to teach you how to make a friend.

同学们早。今天早上我们完成了一次很棒的"检查自己"！现在我来教教你们如何交朋友。

I know meeting new people can be difficult. We don't know if they'll like us or want to be friends.

我知道跟陌生人打交道会很困难。我们不知道他们会不会喜欢我们，会不会想要成为我们的朋友。

Understand that not everyone will want to be friends.
Whenever you see someone that you may want to befriend,
you should go to them and introduce yourself to them.

你要明白不是每个人都会想成为你的朋友。当你见到想要
认识的朋友，你要去跟他们介绍你自己。

An introduction means, you say, "hello and tell the person your name". When you do this, you should look the person in the eye or make eye contact. When you make eye contact and say hello and your name, you extend your hand to shake hands with that person.

自我介绍的意思是说"你好"并告诉那个人你的名字。当你这么做的时候，你要看着对方的眼睛，对准视线。当你们互视，问候并告诉了名字以后，你要伸出手去跟那个人握手。

Then you wait for the person to extend their hand, say "hi", and their name.

然后，要等那个人伸出手来握你的手，问候"你好"并告诉你他的名字。

Afterwards, you may want to invite them to do something with you or just make an introduction. For example, if you're on a playground, you might ask them to play ball, swing, slide, or just play with you. If you're in class, you might ask them to read with you or sit with you during lunch!

随后，你可以邀请他们一起去做点什么，或者就做好自我介绍。例如，如果你在游乐场里，你可以问他们要不要一起踢球，荡秋千，滑滑梯，或者一起玩耍。如果你在教室里，你可以问他们要不要一起读书，或者吃午饭的时候坐在一起。

Now Timmy, will you come up and help me demonstrate or act it out?

现在，可不可以请提米过来帮我示范或者演出来这一段？

Alright class, Timmy and I have showed you how to make a
friend. Now you try it.

好了同学们，我和提米给大家示范了怎么交朋友。现在
该你们试试了。

I'm happy that my classmates and I learned how to make a friend. Don't forget to join me for my next Exciting, Social & Emotional Adventure!